A

LITTLE IN

A WOMAN'S
LITTLE INSTRUCTION BOOK

JASMINE BIRTLES

B**XTREE

First published in Great Britain in 1995 by Boxtree Limited,
Broadwall House, 21 Broadwall, London SE1 9PL

Copyright © by Jasmine Birtles

10 9

ISBN: 0 7522 0182 4

A CIP catalogue entry for this book is available from the British Library.

Cover design by Flash and Associates.

**Printed and bound in the United Kingdom by
The Bath Press, Bath**

FOREWORD

Aren't men wonderful? What would we do without them? But what can we do with them? Who knows what's going on in their minds? Certainly not me, which, of course, is why I put this book together. As you can tell, the information in this tome is founded on a scientific basis of ignorance, confusion and sheer prejudice. It is culled from the experiences of many women – particularly my friends – and from a few of the lovely males who have brightened my life. Please enjoy this book, and if it adversely affects your relationship with your favourite human pet I will, of course, deny all responsibility.

Never do housework.
No man ever made love to a woman
because the house was spotless.

• • •

Don't trust a man who says he's single
and then picks you up in a Volvo Estate
with a child seat in the back.

It's better to have loved a short man
than never to have loved a tall.

• • •

You know he's lying
if his lips are moving.

Remember, you are known by
the idiot you accompany.

• • •

Don't get a man, get a cat –
they don't hog the duvet and
they don't snore.

Have an affair – break up the monogamy.

• • •

Don't imagine you can change a man –
unless he's in nappies.

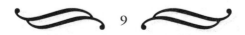

So many men –
so few machine guns.

• • •

If you love a man, set him free.
If he comes back it means he's
forgotten his sandwiches.

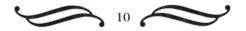

What do you do if your boyfriend walks out?
You shut the door.

• • •

So many men – so many reasons not to
sleep with any of them.

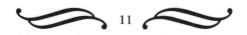

If they can put a man on the moon they
should be able to put them all there.

• • •

Husbands are like children – they're fine
if they're someone else's.

Beware a man who says he believes in equality –
he's about to quit his job.

• • •

Tell him you're not his type –
you have a pulse.

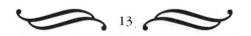

Always remind your husband that the
wages of sin is alimony.

• • •

Wait for the right man to come along
but in the meantime have fun with some
wrong ones.

 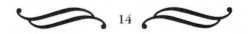

Never let your man's mind wander –
it's too little to be let out alone.

• • •

One of the surest signs that a woman is in
love is that she's divorced her husband.

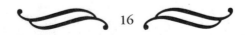

There is only one thing that keeps
most women from being happily married –
their husbands.

• • •

The only reason men are on this planet is
that vibrators can't dance or buy drinks.

Never sleep with a man who's
named his willy.

• • •

Don't even consider divorcing
a Mafia hit-man.

You will find everything you need to
know about a man in his pants drawer.

• • •

If you want a nice man go for a bald one –
they try harder.

If he won't wear a condom, staple the
end of his willy. That'll make him think.

• • •

Never make passes at men with
full glasses.

 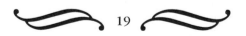 19

Don't expect to find a sensitive and
caring life partner in a man who reads
'Soldier of Fortune.'

• • •

Marrying a man just because you want a
diamond ring shows a lack of depth.

A man who thinks you should be thinner,
and tells you so, should be operated on
without an anaesthetic.

• • •

Go for younger men. You might as well –
they never mature anyway.

A man who can dress himself
without looking like Wurzel Gummidge
is unquestionably gay.

• • •

If he clips his toenails over the living
room floor, shave your armpits over his
copy of *Classic Car*.

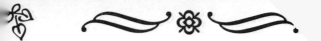

Men who say they like simple foods mean
they like food in easy-to-open packages.

• • •

Don't bother going to the chiropractor
to get rid of a pain in the neck.
Just divorce him.

more than one wife is bigamy.
Having more than one husband is pure insanity.

• • •

Men are all the same - they just have different faces so you can tell them apart.

24

If he says he's leaving you to see the
world, buy him a map.

• • •

Never marry a man for money.
You'll have to earn every penny.

Always remember, you can't be treated
like a doormat if you don't lie down.

• • •

A man's idea of housework:
putting the toilet seat down.

A man's idea of cooking:
phoning the pizza delivery company.

• • •

Definition of a bachelor:
a man who has missed the opportunity to
make some woman miserable.

Don't wake up grumpy in the morning –
let him sleep.

• • •

What's the difference between a husband
and a lover? Day and night.

Definition of a husband:
one who stands by his wife in
troubles she'd never have had if
she hadn't married him.

Women don't make fools of men – most
of the them are the do-it-yourself types.

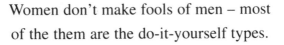

The best reason to divorce a man is a
health reason: you've got sick of him.

Definition of widowhood: the only good
thing some women get out of marriage.

• • •

Always take disappointments like a man –
blame them on a woman.

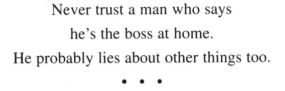

Never trust a man who says
he's the boss at home.
He probably lies about other things too.

• • •

A woman's work that is never done is the
stuff she asked her husband to do.

Men are like buses –
they never appear when you want
them to and when they do they're
'Learner Driver Only'.

Why do women have such a sense of humour?
So that they can appreciate the jokes they married.

● ● ●

Always remember that with men,
no good turn goes unpunished.

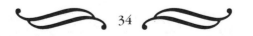

If you think the way to a man's heart is
through his stomach you're aiming too high.

• • •

Why do men fart in bed?
Well, farting in the office is rude isn't it?

If he enjoys flower-arranging,
cares about clothes, and worships
Judy Garland – trust me,
he's not just playing hard to get.

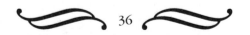

If it has tyres or testicles
it'll be trouble.

• • •

A man's best friend is his sofa.

Advice for brides:
keep the bouquet and throw the
groom away.

• • •

The best way to keep a husband
is in doubt.

Don't waste time trying to find a
man's inner child. You'll have enough to
do coping with his outer one.

• • •

The best way to get a man to do something
is to suggest they're too old for it.

39

Divorce:
nature's way of recycling.

Never buy a water bed if you're married.
You'll just drift apart.

Retirement means twice as much husband
for half as much money.

• • •

Hiring an assassin means never having to
say you're sorry.

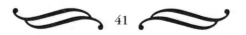

Love is blind but marriage is
a real eye-opener.

• • •

A bad man is like a mortgage – the interest
is unwelcome and the demands never end.

Make sure the man you live with
has a large bum – then you'll always have
somewhere to park your bike.

• • •

Men are like old cars – they need a lot of
touching up before they can perform.

Men's brains are like the prison system –
not enough cells per man.

• • •

There are only two four-letter words that
are offensive to men – don't and stop.

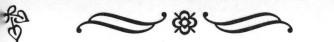

Most men are like old records –
they scratch a lot.

• • •

Never bother to ask a man what his
favourite food is – it's always crumpet.

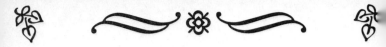

Men are like condoms – they come in three sizes, small, medium and liar.

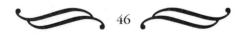

You know your man has insomnia if he keeps waking up every few days.

Don't ask a man to make you some toast –
most can't find the recipe.

• • •

If you wanted a committed man,
look in a mental hospital.

The safest sex is no sex at all –
looking at most men, this is not difficult.

• • •

The real meaning of P.M.T.:
Putting up with Men's Tediousness.

You know your marriage has
lost its glamour when
you find your husband actually *reading*
the articles in Playboy.

Double your storage space –
get rid of your boyfriend.

• • •

Don't buy him men's cosmetics –
there's nothing more effective than a paper bag.

Don't waste your time with a man,
get a monkey – at least *they*
are affectionate and can
be trained to take out the rubbish.

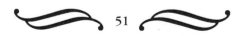

Husbands and dogs have the
same attitude to housework –
they both run away when the
vacuum cleaner appears.

One good reason for marrying
a man is that most of them
are quite a bargain –
in fact they're really cheap.

Beware the strong, silent type –
he has nothing to say.

• • •

A man in bed is like microwave food –
30 seconds and he's done.

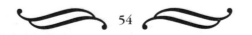

Make the bed after a
one night stand –
you don't want him to think
you're a slut do you?

Most living organisms
need a clean environment to grow –
except bacteria, insects
and men.

Don't be impressed
by a man who says he's in the S.A.S. –
it stands for
Slappers And Slags.

The Children of Israel wandered
round the desert for 40 years.
Even in biblical times men wouldn't ask
for directions.

Don't be impressed by
sporting victories –
unless he has won
the three-legged race on his own.

For the last time... *he's never going to leave her!*

• • •

If he says his wife doesn't understand him tell him to speak slower.

Don't go out with rugby players –
they think pointy balls are normal.

• • •

Don't go out with football players –
they're always dribbling in their shorts.

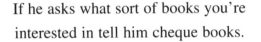

If he asks what sort of books you're
interested in tell him cheque books.

• • •

A married man is a single man with the
nerve extracted.

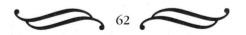

They say marriage is a lottery but at least
in lotteries you have a chance.

• • •

If he tells you he likes black underwear,
stop washing his pants.

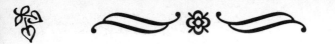

Beware a man who says he can drive you
mad – he's probably got rabies.

• • •

Beware a man who says he has no
enemies – all his friends hate him.

Be tolerant of men –
after all, it's just ninety-nine per cent
of them that give the other one per cent
a bad name.

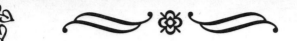

If you want commitment marry a whale –
they mate for life.

• • •

If you can't find a man get a yoghurt –
at least they have culture.

You know you're on a bad date when he
excuses himself to call the wife.

• • •

Never hit a man when he's down,
he might get up again.

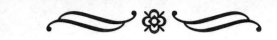

Men can't think straight because they
always have curves on their mind.

• • •

Married men make good salesmen because
they're used to lying.

Every woman should have a husband –
preferably her own.

• • •

By the time most men learn how to
behave themselves they are too old to be
able to do anything else.

Marrying a man for his looks is like
buying a house for its paint.

• • •

Remind your husband that no woman has ever
shot a man while he was doing the dishes.

When a woman is looking for a husband
she is either single or married.

• • •

Give a man an inch and he'll say it's ten.

There are three kinds of men:
the intelligent, the handsome and
the majority.

• • •

If you want him to remember your
anniversary, get married on his birthday.

Don't bother with a man who gets
junk mail that starts,
'You may already be a loser...'

• • •

Don't bother with a man who gets cut off
by the Samaritans.

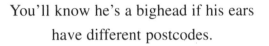

You'll know he's a bighead if his ears
have different postcodes.

• • •

Avoid religious men who start
their prayers with
'Dear God, do you need anything?'

The average man has two main problems –
he thinks everyone else is better than him
and so do they.

• • •

A man's idea of serious commitment is
usually, 'Oh all right, I'll stay the night.'

Men are like flight balloons –
they're both full of hot air.

• • •

If you want a dog get a retriever –
to stop your man getting away.

Men are like snowmen except that you get
more warmth from a snowman.

• • •

Most men are like the Brazilian rain forest –
pretty dense.

Boring men are like snot –
they get up your nose.

• • •

Hooray Henrys are like tinned mushrooms –
cultivated but no taste.

Don't just *think* about divorce,
get yourself featured in 'Hello'.

Artistic men are like orbiting satellites,
except that satellites are more down-to-earth.

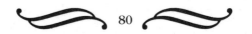

If you want to meet a truly annoying man,
go to a whine bar.

• • •

You know a man is sincere if he admits
his lover has more brains than him.

Always wear high heels –
it makes it easier to look down on him.

• • •

Definition of a man of manners –
he gets out of the bath to pee.

Women sleep with men who,
if they were women, they wouldn't even
have bothered to have lunch with.

• • •

Men don't like cats because cats are
cleverer than them.

Love him to death and make sure he's
kept up his life insurance payments.

• • •

Don't allow yourself the excuse that
'love is blind' – wear your glasses!

Men are like houses –
it's nice to own one but at least
if you rent one you know *someone*
will mend the washing machine.

Upper class men are a little
like dishwashers
– they have plenty of Finish but only
the machines actually wash-up.

Don't touch unidentified objects in his sock drawer.

•　•　•

The trouble with women is our trouble with men.

You know you're really in trouble if your
man *and* your TV set aren't working.

• • •

It's easy to handle men if you know how –
the problem is most of us just don't know how.

Don't argue with your husband –
you might win, then you'd be in real trouble.

• • •

Married women don't go out looking for
trouble, they get all they want at home.

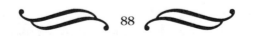

The best way to drive your husband mad
is to smile in your sleep.

• • •

Don't take your problem to bed with you,
unless he refuses to sleep alone.

Never trust love at first sight –
take a second look.

• • •

Whenever you meet a man who would
make a good husband,
you will usually find that he is.

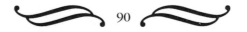

He's not a model husband unless he's a
working one.

• • •

Try to make sure you actually *have*
a relationship before you tell him what's
wrong with his wardrobe.

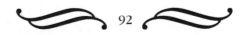

Try to have reached at least
your second date before
suggesting the colour of the curtains
for your nuptial home.

Face it, he *doesn't* want to
talk about where your
relationship's going – he wants to
finish chainsawing the sofa...

If there is a group of men doing *anything* with a ball in a field, another group of men will watch.

• • •

Isn't it strange that men with the name of Francis aren't called Fanny?

What? You want him to talk about his feelings? That's extra - it doesn't come in the list price for a man.

• • •

Men don't use cookbooks - they're too much like directions.

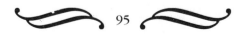

Remember, a sense of humour
does not mean that you tell him jokes,
it means you laugh at his.

• • •

Being intelligent does not mean
you know a lot, it means you make him
think that he does.

Forget the Labours of Hercules,
if he can buy you a months-worth
of sanitary protection in
the local supermarket without flinching,
he's a superhero.

If he has difficulty sleeping
always get into bed saying
"I think we should talk about
our relationship...."

Don't make him come
clothes-shopping with you.
Compared with that most men consider
root-canal work a soft option.

If he asks you if you're faking it
tell him no, you're just practising.

• • •

Sadly, all men are created equal.

When he asks you if he's your first
tell him 'You may be, you look familiar'.

• • •

You know he's putting on weight if he
needs a larger bra than you do.

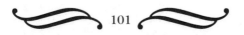

If men knew what pain
they cause when they
don't ring – they probably
still wouldn't bother.

The main point of having a boyfriend
is so that he can one day
graduate to the exalted status of
'a former boyfriend'.

There are two significant influences in a man's life and they are both his mother.

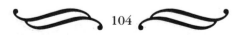

However hard they try, no man has ever looked good in suspenders.

If you need to talk seriously about your
relationship, try putting it in footballing terms.

• • •

Men are useful to have around as they are usually
larger than women and make good windshields.

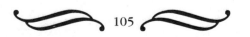

Men are congenitally unable to open
presents without complaining and then
nearly breaking them.

• • •

Men like to chase women
so make it fun for him – hide.

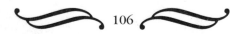

Don't even think about dating a man
who has nicknamed himself
'Master of the Universe'.

• • •

Every woman knows that measurements
are just statistics and statistics always lie.

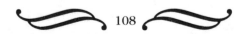

Probably the best reason to
marry a man is that you will get
to use his credit cards.
It's also probably the only reason.

Try and marry a man who already
has daughters your age – they can be
useful when you can't find the right shoes
to match your outfit.

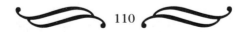

Scientists have just
discovered something that can
do the work of five men –
a woman.

If he is still friends with
his ex-girlfriends, be impressed.
If he sees them all more than he sees you,
be worried.

If you're thinking of marrying
a man take all his ex-girlfriends
out to lunch first –
that'll put you off.

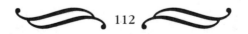

The best reason for having sex –
working off that
extra piece of chocolate fudge cake
you wolfed at dinner.

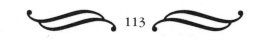

Remember, a man will never give
an honest opinion of your dress
unless he's considering wearing it
himself later.

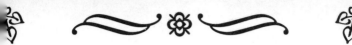

You know things are slacking off
when you don't care where your husband
goes just so long as you don't have
to follow.

Don't sleep with a Porsche driver –
they don't check
to see if you're coming before
they pull out.

Men are like animals –
messy, insensitive and
potentially violent –
but they make great pets.

An unmarried man is an example of the
failure of Care in the Community.

• • •

Only pick up a man in a Supermarket if
his chauffeur is pushing the trolley.

You know he's big-headed if he says he
wants to leave his body to science fiction.

• • •

Never trust a naked milkman.

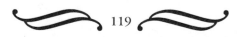

Why do men grow beer guts?
So they'll have somewhere
to rest the pizza
during the big match.

Don't marry a bearded man unless you've
seen a photo of him without it.

• • •

Never date a doctor whose plants are dying.

Never sleep with a man who
fakes foreplay.

• • •

Marriage is like the Financial Times –
no comment.

Men can't play dumb because
it's hard to play at reality.

• • •

Men who wear socks with sandals should
be certified.

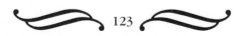

Only ask him what he wants for dinner
if he's buying.

• • •

Marry for money – you're worth it.

There are a lot of words you can use
to describe men – strong, caring, loving –
they'd be wrong but you could
still use them.

Jasmine Birtles is a comedienne, writer, broadcaster and journalist. She currently divides her time between writing and performing comedy material, writing books, producing and presenting radio programmes for BBC Radio 3, 4, and 5 Live and writing for a variety of national newspapers. She has many men friends, and points them to the light and waters them regularly.